100% Loved is your passport to this beautiful keepsake journal. This journal will help create a record of your life and help guide you to express who you are as a person. As time passes, it will be so much fun to look back at your answers. You will get a sense of how your interests and life have changed and grown. Once you have filled in all the writing prompts, you will have a wealth of memories to pass down to your children and their children, a true family keepsake for generations to come.

*To Lois and John
(Mom and Dad)*

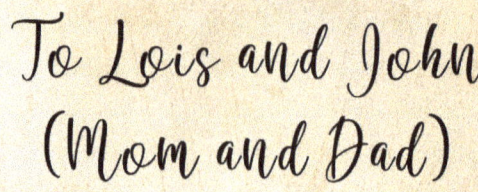

I'M FOREVER GRATEFUL

for giving me my passport to adventure by encouraging play, imagination, taking risks, and learning from mistakes. Your endless love, support, guidance, and being amazing role models will forever be appreciated and remembered.

100% Loved
MY PASSPORT TO ADVENTURE

By John Janezic

Illustrated by Mark Sean Wilson

MANY**SEASONS**PRESS

Mesa, Arizona | 2024

SECOND EDITION

100% Loved, My Passport to Adventure

Copyright © 2024 John Janezic

MANY**SEASONS**PRESS

Published by Many Seasons Press
An Imprint of Multimedia Publishing Project
123 N. Centennial Way, Suite 105
Mesa, Arizona 85201
480-939-9689 | ManySeasonsPress.com

Written by John Janezic
johnnyjroxx@gmail.com | JohnJanezic.com

Illustrated by Mark Sean Wilson
www.markerdoodle.com

Paperback ISBN: 978-1-956203-53-0

Library of Congress Control Number: 2024940290

PASSPORT RULES:

1. Keep this journal forever.

2. If you run out of space writing your answers, look to the back of the journal for extra pages to continue your writing.

3. Be curious, take risks, smile, and keep your imagination loaded and ready to play!

Join the Louie The Roach 100% Loved Club
Every week Louie sends you a positive message along with his famous jokes.
To become a member, send your email address to johnnyjroxx@gmail.com
Louie will put you on his list.

100% L♥ved
MY PASSPORT TO ADVENTURE

Louie dedicates this special journal to the amazing You. Be curious, take risks, and keep your imagination loaded and ready to play. Always give your best effort, but don't forget to take time to laugh and play. The world is a much better place with you in it.

Hello you amazing creature!

This Journal is your passport to adventure, laughter, and lifelong memories. Keep it forever. Look back on it often. Share with family, friends, and your future family. There is a special section in this journal for you to fill out now and when you are older. During your adventure, don't forget to take time to smell the roses and eat lots of toilet paper.

Love, Louie The Roach

Full Name: _____

Nickname: _____

Age: _____

Date: ____/____/_____

Cockroaches have lived on planet Earth for more than 280 million years! In all that time, Louie has heard great advice and learned so much from his relatives and friends. Louie calls that a "Louieism!"

Ism definition: a suffix added to the end of a word to indicate that the represents a specific practice, system, or philosophy.

Louie will be sharing his favorite "isms" throughout the journal!

Louieism : "People will not always remember what you say. People will not always remember what you do. But they will always remember the way you make them feel." *– Maya Angelou*

Write your family's (or your own) favorite "isms"

HERE I AM

If you could pick any other name for yourself, what would it be?

Louieism: "What does it mean to be 100% Loved?" Love who you are, flaws and all, so you can support others who aren't quite there yet.

YOU ARE NEVER ALONE

Write down all the things you love! This can be anything big, small, or unique.

_____

_____

_____

_____

What words would you use to describe yourself?

_____, _____, _____, _____.

*Louie loves to dance! He builds awesome forts and has a fun, creative imagination.

Find three or more things you really like about yourself. (It could be your perfect handwriting, your hair, your long eyelashes, or your smile).

Brag about yourself!

_____

_____

_____

_____

_____

_____

You meet a really cool genie who grants you three wishes. What do you wish for?

A. _____

B. _____

C. _____

If you could ask any animal, insect, or reptile a question, what animal would it be and what question would you ask?

_____

_____

_____

_____

_____

_____

How do you like to help others?

_____

_____

_____

What's a memory that makes you happy?

_____

_____

_____

_____

4

When I am older, I want to be a...

----

*Louie the Roach loves toilet paper! Here is a poem about toilet paper from Louie.

Toilet paper, toilet paper, soft and white
Eating you just seems so right
Toilet paper, toilet paper, in my belly
Not with peanut butter but only with jelly

Louie the Roach

IT'S YOUR TURN. MAKE UP YOUR OWN POEM ABOUT TOILET PAPER!

Write the poem here:

LIST NICE THINGS PEOPLE HAVE SAID ABOUT YOU.

LET'S TALK

The greatest present I ever received is_____

If you started talking in your sleep, what are you afraid you would say?

My favorite band or singer is...

Here are some of my favorite song titles:

How long does it take you to get ready in the morning?

What food(s) do you find disgusting?

What is your favorite Halloween costume?

My favorite holiday is_____because

My favorite book is...

My favorite movie is...

My favorite cartoon character is...

The best day of the week is_____because

Louieism:"The best way to make friends is to be friendly, helpful, and be yourself."

Louie's Rules for Being a Good Friend

A. Be a good listener.
B. Be supportive, honest, and trustworthy.
C. Sometimes friends get angry, and that's ok, just be sure to work out the problem and make up.

Which friends would you trust with your deepest secrets?

--------------------   --------------------

--------------------   --------------------

My favorite thing to play at recess is...

What makes a great playground?

Who is your current crush?

What do you like about them?

Do they know you have a crush on them?

What slang terms are popular now? Write the term and meaning. Example: LOL (Laugh out loud) or GOAT (Greatest of all time)

_____ (_____)
_____ (_____)
_____ (_____)

Louie's Poem about his Favorite People

My favorite people make me smile
They cheer me up, love me, and have a unique style.

There are times we may not always agree
But they will always have my back, that's a guarantee.

My favorite people are the best!
I say that loud while beating my chest!

-Louie the Roach

Imagination Loaded:
Where creativity comes to life

Imagination Loaded:
Where creativity comes to life

Who are your favorite people in the world and why are they your favorite people in the world?

Thank you Notes...

Everyone loves to get handwritten notes and letters, especially when they come as a surprise! Let's write one now!

Think of a teacher, friend, family member, mom, dad, grandparent, or anyone else, and tell them why you are grateful to have them in your life. Tell them what you like about them. You can either mail it to that person or hand deliver it to them! Use the extra journal pages to keep track of who you sent letters to and why.

Use this page to write a letter to your future self. Tell yourself your hopes, dreams, and goals.

MY AMAZING, COOL, WEIRD, FAMILY

Louieism: "A family is not only connected by blood, but by joy, laughter, and respect for each other." -Richard Bach

Ask your grandma, grandpa, mom, dad, or any other relative for their favorite recipe. Write it here and keep it alive for future generations to come.

_____

_____

_____

_____

_____

_____

More delicious recipes!

- -

- -

- -

- -

- -

Imagination Loaded:
Where creativity comes to life

Imagination Loaded:
Where creativity comes to life

My fun story

Ask your mom or dad for memorable things you have said when you were younger. What was your first word, first sentence, funniest, smartest or wackiest thing you said? Use the information to create a fun story or your own comic.

Comic Title

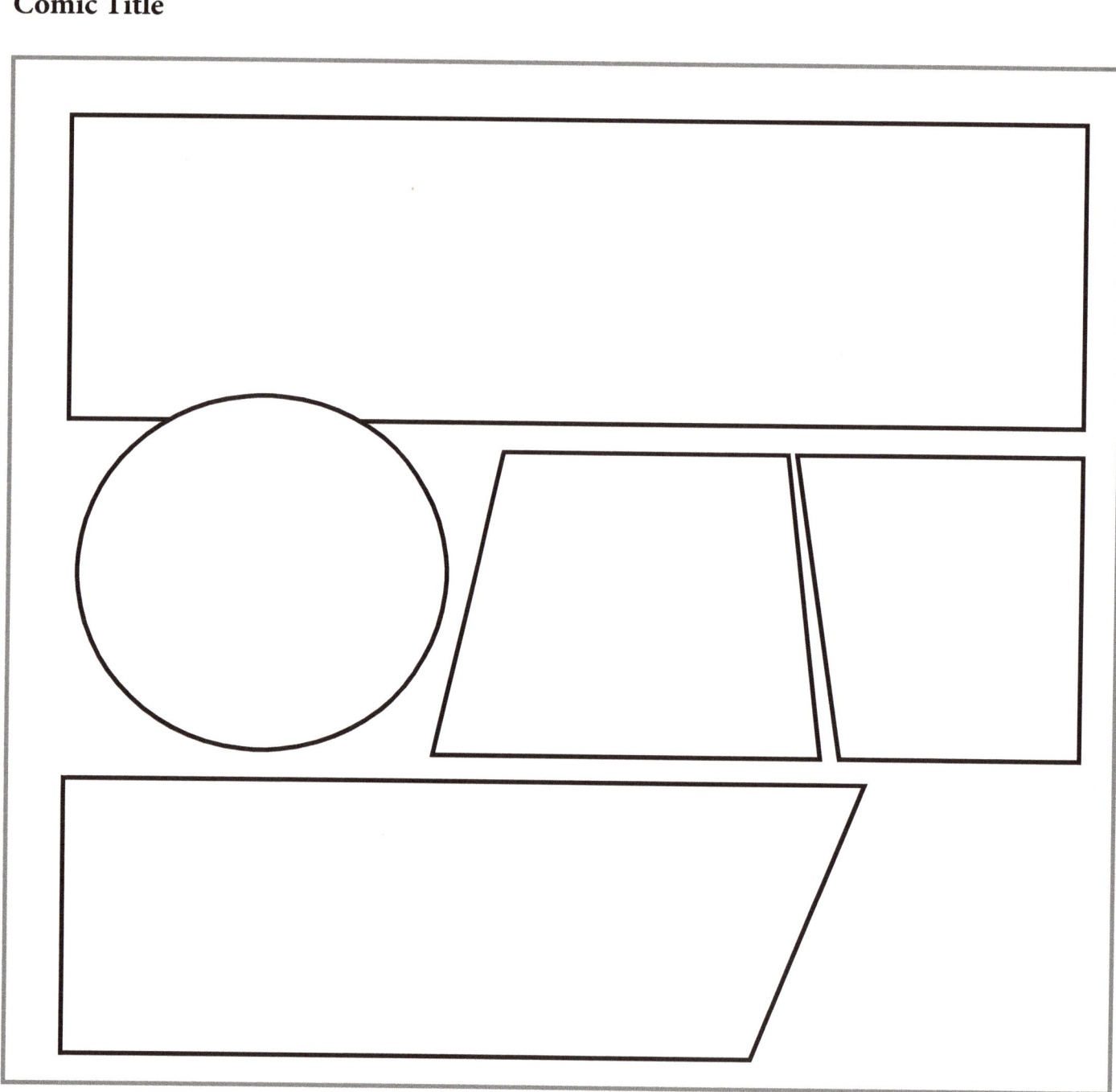

I have _____brothers

I have_____sisters

Ask your brothers and sisters to write something special about you or what they love about you!

--- --

My favorite place to go as a family is...

(don't forget to write why it is your favorite family place)

Roach on Wheels

Here are my favorite games I love playing with my family...

(board games, video games or any other games you play)

My family has these fun traditions...

--- --

------- --

--------- --

I have_____ pets

Here are my favorite pet memories

--- ---

--------------- ---

--------------- ---

-------------------------- --

------------------------------------- -----------------------------

Where is the best place to play in my neighborhood?

What do you think your parents will do when you're older and move out of the house?

Interview questions for grandparents or other special relatives...

(Write the answers here or use the additional blank pages at the end of your journal. Interview as many relatives as you want. These will be cherished answers when you are older).

Name? _____

When and where were you born?

_____/_____/_____ ____:_____

_____

How did your parents choose your name?

Did you have any nicknames?

Did you have pets? What kind?

What were your favorite foods as a kid?

What were your favorite and least favorite subjects in school?

What kind of games did you play growing up?

What did you want to be when you grew up?

Where was your favorite place to go on vacation?

Did you like to play sports?

What was your first job?

How did you meet your spouse?

How did you get engaged?

What do you remember most about your wedding day?

_____

_____

_____

_____

What's been your favorite age to be and why?

_____

_____

_____

Looking back at your life, what are you most proud of?

_____

_____

_____

Favorite food to cook. May I please have the recipe?

_____

_____

What would I be surprised to learn about you?

_____

_____

Louie's Family Bonding Fun

Time to Eat!

Time to have weekend fun and create memories. Gather the family, along with an old family recipe. If you don't have one, look for a delicious bread or cookie recipe.

VOLUNTEER TOGETHER

Family quality time! You spend the day with your family, experience the joy of helping others, and together make the world a better place.

When volunteering, consider a food bank, animal shelter, visit a nursing home, or send cards/letters to our military troops. What ever you choose, find a shared passion, and make it your family's volunteer project. Every state has charity and volunteer lists online, so ask your parents and siblings to help in your search.

Let's Read: Family Book-Club!

Choose stories that appeal to all family members, no matter their age. Charlie and the Chocolate Factory, Jumanji, or Because Cockroaches Rule (I had to throw that one in!) These

books contain humor adults can enjoy, too. Maybe have one person read aloud or take turns so that you can experience the story unfolding together. With older kids, establish a schedule so everyone has reading time before your family meeting to discuss the book or check out multiple copies from the library. After you have finished, see if there is a movie that goes along with the book. Have a family movie night and discuss the similarities and/or differences between the book and the movie.

Improvisation and Sparking Imagination

Louie loves performing improvisation and being in plays. Here are some of his favorite theatre games. This is fun for family and friends! Start your own neighborhood drama club!

(TMATTY) TELL ME ABOUT THE TIME YOU

This hilarious improvisation game is played by the whole family or a group of friends. Someone starts the game by standing

(center stage) in front of family or friends. A member of the family or friends asks the person, "Tell me about the time you..." and this is where it gets fun. Finishing the sentence with something fun and crazy. For example...

TELL ME ABOUT THE TIME YOU

- ✔ Fell out of an airplane
- ✔ Went camping and saw a lion
- ✔ Ate dog food
- ✔ Performed as a clown in a circus
- ✔ Visited Mars
- ✔ Ate 75 hot dogs in a contest
- ✔ Were a secret agent
- ✔ Broke both legs
- ✔ Got an F in PE class
- ✔ Wrestled an alligator
- ✔ Had a jelly fish sting you

Ok, you get the idea. The person answering must come up with a beginning, middle, and end to the story. The story should not take long, maybe 1-2 minutes, but they need to start the story as soon as they get their TMATTY. At the end of the story, take a bow and the next person goes up. You will be surprised how fast you can make up a really cool story!

TELL ME ABOUT THE TIME YOU

(List your own ideas)

WORLD'S WORST

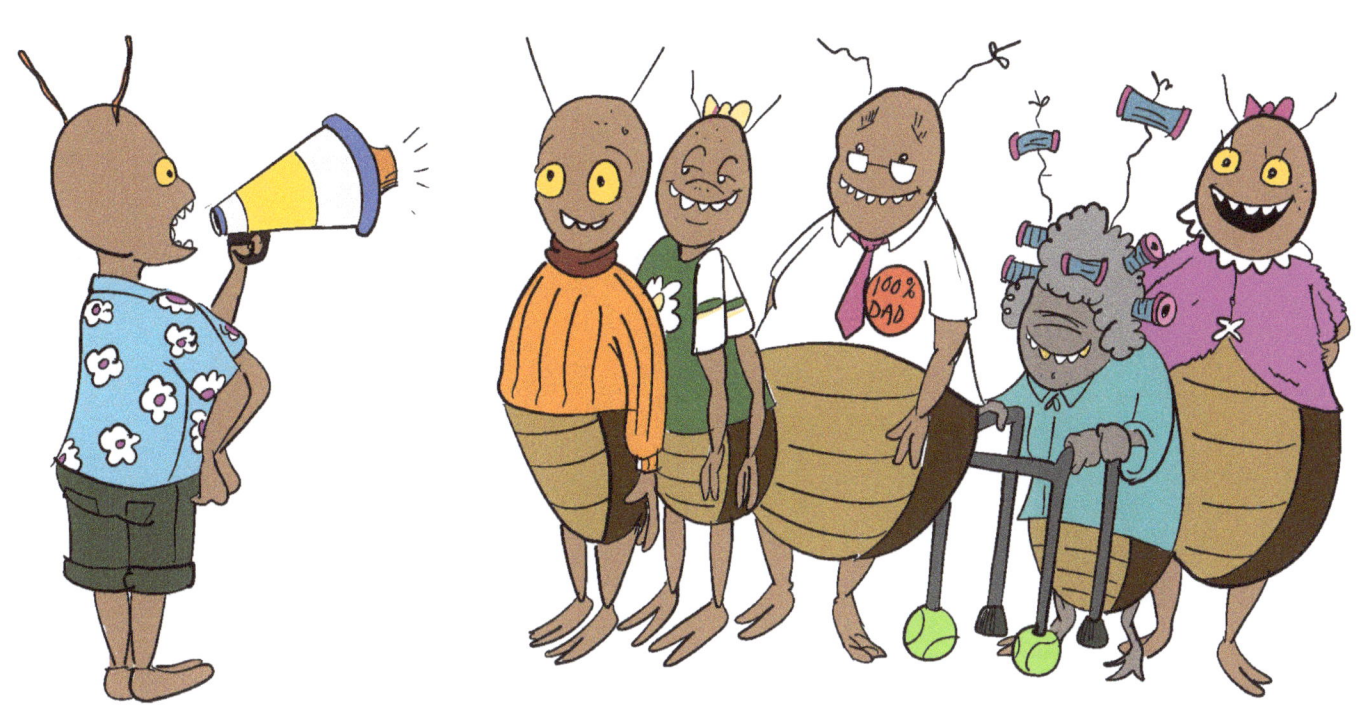

A. Your family and/or friends all stand in a line facing the person who will be the caller. The caller sits away from the people in line.

B. The caller gives out an occupation, famous person, tv commercial, or situation (wedding, funeral, family reunion).

C. Now anyone can come out of the line, take center stage and give their world's worst of whatever was asked. The response should be short and to the point.

D. As soon as you are done, go back in line. Hopefully people will keep coming out. As one person leaves someone else should be coming out. You don't need to take turns, anyone can go at any time.

Change the **World's Worst** suggestion every 4 or 5 performances

Example: World's Worst...Uber Driver—someone comes out and says,

"Hi, I'm your Uber driver, I'm new to this city. I don't really know where anything is... but I'll do my best!"

World's Worst thing to say at a wedding...

"That's the smallest diamond I have ever seen."

You can Google World's Worst improvisation game to read suggestions and watch videos on how to play this game. Write your suggestions below.

QUESTIONS THAT MAKE YOU GO HMMM

 How can cockroaches live up to a week without their heads?

 Why doesn't glue stick to the inside of the bottle?

When you forget a thought, where does it go?

 Why does the Easter Bunny bring eggs when rabbits don't lay eggs?

 Can a fish get seasick?

Now it's your turn, write some questions that make you go hmmm.

--?
--?
--?
--?
--?
--?
--?
--?
--?
--?
--?

Fears...

For one-week, list fears or something that makes you nervous or negative. Then challenge yourself by answering these questions:

A. What can you do to reduce your fear in this situation?

B. What would you tell your friend who had the same fear?

C. List a positive thought to your negative thought.

List fears here...

Questions to answer Now and in the Future

Answer NOW

Answer in 20 YEARS
(Give or Take)

My crush is

How do you see yourself
in the future?

The best joke I ever heard
is...

How will you continue to
encourage yourself if
times get tough?

How many kids do you
imagine having? What are
their names?

What does the world look
like now?

What would you like to say
say to your future self?

My crush is

How do you see yourself
in the future?

The best joke I ever heard
is...

How will you continue to
encourage yourself if
times get tough?

Do you have kids now?
What are their names?

What does the world look
like now?

What would you like to say
say to your younger self?

Imagination Loaded:
Where creativity comes to life

Imagination Loaded:
Where creativity comes to life

LOUIE'S AMAZING AND STUPENDOUS TRICKS TO AMAZE YOUR FAMILY AND FRIENDS

Louie's Bewildering Mind Reading Deception

Deception tools needed:
Pencil and paper

A. Take the piece of paper and pre-write NO on it but make sure the person does not see that.

B. Find a friend, family member, or teacher.

C. Tell them to pick a number between 1 and 500. Next tell them you have already written down what they will say on your piece of paper.

D. You say, "Is it 283!"

E. They will say **"NO"**

hopefully, I mean what is the chance they will say 283?!)

F. Then show them the paper with NO written on it.

Your friends will be amazed at your awesome mind reading abilities!!

Louie's Bewildering Rock and Roll Magic Trick

Rock and Roll Magic Trick Tools Needed: Small Rock and a Cup

A. Find someone who will enjoy an amazing trick.

B. Tell them, "The great (say your name) will now amaze you by getting this rock out from under this cup without touching the cup!" *(Or anything fun you can think of saying)*

C. Now put the rock under the cup.

D. Next, create the best look of concentration you can do. Really stare at the cup. Don't say a word. Total concentration is important here!

E. After you have concentrated long enough. Proudly and loudly announce, "OK, it...is...GONE!!"

F. Tell your friend to lift the cup and see for yourself.

G. As soon as they lift the cup, take the rock and remove it!! *(Don't touch the cup)*

Stand up and take your well-deserved BOW!!!

Louie's Mind-Boggling Wall or Door Feat

Stunt tools needed: A friend and either a door or wall

A. Have a friend go up to the nearest wall or door.

B. Have them put their right foot *(length wise) and right ear against the wall or door.*

C. Then tell them to lift their left foot off the floor and hold it in the air.

There is no way they will be able to do this. Impossible!!
(If they can, take a video and send it to me: johnnyjroxx@gmail.com)

Louie's Really Weird but Cool Stunt

A. Sit in a chair and make sure you have both feet on the ground.

B. Lift up your right foot and move it in a circle. Clockwise Circle.
(*Very important that it is clockwise*)

C. While moving your foot in a circle, draw the number 6 in the air with your right hand.

D. Your foot will start to change direction as you draw the 6!! Try it with friends and family!

Let the laughs begin.

LOUIE'S FAVORITE MATH PROBLEM

A. Write this equation down and show it to someone.

$$5+5+5=550$$

B. Challenge someone to add ONE LINE to the problem to make it true.

C. Make sure you tell the person that adding a line through the equal sign is not an option.

D. Look at the first plus sign. Put a line to make it vertical. This will change the plus sign into a 4.

Answer: $5 \ 4 \ 5+5=550$

Loading Your Imagination

Build Your Own Telephone...
Plus learn how sound travels

Supplies Needed:

- ☐ *2 Cans (metal soup or bean cans work best)*
- ☐ *String*
- ☐ *Paper Clips*
- ☐ *Hammer (make sure you get an adult to help you)*
- ☐ *Small Nail*

A. Wash the empty cans. *(unless you want beans in your ears)*

B. Turn the cans upside down and use the hammer and nail to punch a small hole at the bottom of each can.
(Don't forget to ask an adult for help with this)

C. Cut a long piece of string.

D. Thread one end through the hole and into the can.

E. Tie the end to a paper clip.

F. Pull the string from the outside until the paper clip is flat on the bottom inside the can.

G. Repeat this with the other end of the string and the paper clip.

Your phone is now ready to use!

How does your amazing, cool, old school, phone work? The sound of your voice vibrates the can and this causes the string to vibrate. Our ears collect the sound vibration, send them to our brain, then we hear the sound! How awesome is that?!

LEMONADE STAND

Earn money for vacation or something fun!

Supplies Needed:
- [ ] *1 ½ cups freshly squeezed lemon juice or you can use the bottled juice too.*
- [ ] *5 cups cold water*
- [ ] *1 ½ cups sugar*
- [ ] *2 lemons for garnish*
- [ ] *Ice*

1. Combine lemon juice, water, and sugar into a large pitcher and stir until sugar is completely dissolved.

2. Dump lemon slices onto the top of the lemonade.

3. Top with ice to keep it nice and cold.

4. You can add a pinch of salt to the lemonade to make it tastier. Try it and see if you like it better!

SPLASH AND COOL OFF...

Great way to cool off in the summer!

SPONGE FIGHT:

A. Get some friends together.
B. Soak lots of small sponges in buckets of cold water.
C. Run around and throw them at each other.

MINI-SHOWER...

A. Punch a bunch of holes in the bottom of a clean gallon or half gallon milk carton.
B. Take it outside.
C. Fill it with cold water and quickly hold it over your head! Ahhh, doesn't that feel great?!

WATER SLIDE...

A. Get a big sheet of plastic. *(A plastic drop cloth works fine)*
B. Lay it on the ground and spray water all over it. Or have a hose near the top with water constantly running down the plastic.
C. Sit down and slide on it feet first or slide on your stomach arms first!

NEIGHBORHOOD FUN...
SWEATER RELAY RACE

A. Get a group of friends and divide them into two equal teams.

B. Give each team a sweater.

C. The first runner for each team puts on the sweater, buttons it, runs to the finish line, unbuttons it, and runs back.

D. The sweater is given to the next team member who does the exact same thing.

E. The winning team is the one who finishes first.

Try to find sweaters with lots of buttons.

THE FAMOUS NEIGHBORHOOD PARADE

A. Decorate bikes, trikes, big wheels, wagons, and anything else you can think of.

B. Weave strips of crepe paper through the spokes of the bike tires. Use flags, streamers, and anything else fun to decorate the items for the big parade!

C. Music: Parades are more fun with music. You can ring bells, beat on boxes, bang pots and pans *(ask a parent if this is ok,)* and hum through paper towel tubes.

D. Costumes: Friends who belong to scouting groups can wear their uniforms, favorite Halloween costumes, old clothes, and painted faces are a blast!

E. Special Attractions: Do you have a pet that is willing to be in the parade? *(Make sure it is in a cage or on a leash)*

F. Anything else fun you can think of adding.

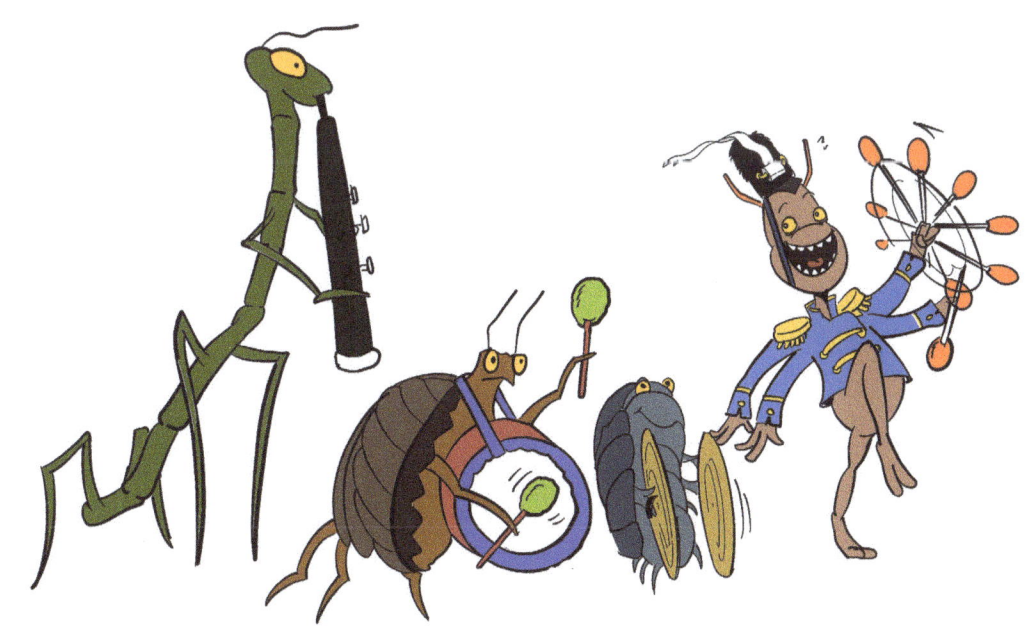

Louie's Private Joke Collection

Did you know that trees poop? Have you ever seen a number 2 pencil?!

What do you call someone who refuses to fart in public? A Private Tutor!

Why did the toilet paper not cross the road? Because it was stuck in the crack!

Who are the most dangerous farters in the world? Ninjas. They're silent but deadly!

Do you know what Mary had when she went out to dinner? Everyone knows "Mary had a little lamb."

What do you get when you cross a pig and a centipede? Bacon and Legs!

What's the difference between boogers and broccoli? Kids don't eat broccoli!

What do you call two monkeys sharing an Amazon Account? PRIME-mates!

Why does E.T. have such big eyes? Because he saw his phone bill!
(Watch the movie E.T. if you have not seen it)

What happened when the King's Men played a joke on Humpty Dumpty? He fell for it!

What can you do to make the world 100% Loved?

Don't forget to send me pictures or videos of you or your family having fun with the activities laid out in the journal.

johnnyjroxx@gmail.com

CONTINUE ON JOURNALING

YOUR PERSONAL NOTEBOOK

_____

"COLOR ME AND CUT ME OUT AND YOU TOO CAN BECOME MEEEEEEE!!!!!!!"

ITEMS NEEDED TO CREATE YOUR OWN COLORED LOUIE MASK

CRAYONS,
POPSICLE STICK,
SCISSORS, AND
LOUIE'S FAVORITE. GLUE!

"LET'S GET COLORING!!!"